Animal Stories
from the
Bible

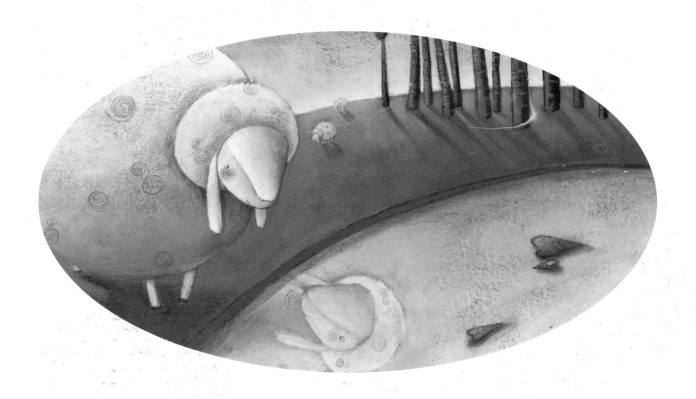

Retold by Lois Rock
Illustrated by Martina Peluso

LION
CHILDREN'S

For Arturo   M.P.

Text by Lois Rock
Illustrations copyright © 2011 Martina Peluso
This edition copyright © 2011 Lion Hudson

The moral rights of the author and illustrator
have been asserted

A Lion Children's Book
an imprint of
Lion Hudson plc
Wilkinson House, Jordan Hill Road,
Oxford OX2 8DR, England
www.lionhudson.com
ISBN 978 0 7459 6220 7

First edition 2011
1 3 5 7 9 10 8 6 4 2

A catalogue record for this book is available
from the British Library

Typeset in 18/23 Lapidary 333 BT
Printed in China January 2012 (manufacturer LH06)

Distributed by:
UK: Marston Book Services Ltd, PO Box 269, Abingdon, Oxon OX14 4YN
USA: Trafalgar Square Publishing, 814 N Franklin Street, Chicago, IL 60610
USA Christian Market: Kregel Publications, PO Box 2607, Grand Rapids, MI 49501

Contents

The Snake's Story

The Garden of Eden

Shhh! Lissssten! This is a story as old as time.

It is not my own story. I am only the storyteller. I heard the tale when I was young and am telling it to you so that you in turn may pass it on – for, dear listeners, it must never be forgotten.

Now, everything in it happened at the very beginning. Out of the empty nothing God made a world: bright blue heaven, dark brown earth, seas that glittered emerald and silver under a bright golden sun.

Seeds began to grow, their first leaves opening like a baby's hands but growing into the most marvellous plants: flowers, vegetables, trees, creepers. I'm quite fond of creepers – are you?

Then God made living things: the fish that slip and splash in the water; the birds that soar through the air, trilling, tweeting, cawing, croaking. And animals: every kind of creature you can think of and more besides; there are some that you have not even discovered, they hide so secretively in hole and hollow.

Finally, people. Yes, people like you. This tale is about the first two: the man was Adam and the woman was Eve. God treated them as his special friends. God had made everything and God had made it all very, very lovely, but it seemed that God liked people best.

God planted them a garden to live in. It was a paradise. The trees were sometimes a dancing mass of blossom – pink and white and frothy; other times their branches stooped under their harvest of fruit: red, gold, purple, luscious. Adam and Eve had everything they wanted.

Well, to be fair, every living thing had everything it needed; when God made the world, he made it very well. But Adam and Eve were so sure they had God's extra special favour. And the snake, the wisest of creatures, saw a tiny little chance to make them a bit more… humble.

The snake went and whispered to Eve, "Is it true that you can eat the fruit of any tree in this garden?"

"Yes," she replied, hardly pausing from munching on something delicious. "Except for one. God told us that if we touch its fruit, it will kill us. I'm not even interested in going to look at it."

"Sss, sss, sss," giggled that cunning snake. "God can be so sneaky. It won't harm you! It will make you wise! As wise as God!"

That got Eve thinking. In the end, she couldn't resist. She went and picked some of the fruit and tasted it.

"This is good," she called to Adam. "Come and try this. It's unlike anything else."

It was unlike anything else. When Adam and Eve ate the fruit, it opened their eyes to bad things as well as good. Trouble was not long in arriving.

That evening, God found out and God was both angry and sad. There's a lovely word for that: wrath. God's wrath is something to behold.

God told Adam and Eve that they could no longer dwell in paradise. They must go out into the real world. There among thorns and thistles they must make their own living. Grow their own vegetables. Catch their own food. Until the day they died.

So they did. From that day forward, people and snakes have been enemies. And that's why the story must never be forgotten – for it reminds you and me alike what misery it is for every living thing that evil came into the world.

The Raven's Story

Noah and the Flood

Craa. I always have a croaky voice. It's not the best for storytelling, but as you're here, I'll do what I can. I always think my story gets overlooked.

It's in the Bible, you know – part of the story of the flood. I saw it all.

I saw just how wicked people had become. They were wicked to me too, you know: throwing stones and hurling insults whenever I came near their fields. I don't do any harm, but I think my looks count against me. And my voice, of course. Craa.

Anyway, God was displeased with every act of wickedness. Washing the whole lot of them away in a great torrent didn't seem a bad idea to me. Drastic, of course, but those crooks would probably have destroyed themselves if God hadn't done something.

In fact, I think God wanted to give goodness a chance. That's why he chose Noah to build a huge ark on which every life form

11

would survive. It's a miracle to me how Noah and his family ever finished it. But they did. And they welcomed two of every living creature on board.

I was so glad to be one of the pair of ravens. I felt glad to be under a roof as the rain came hissing down. I know what it's like to be out in a downpour, sitting there hunched and bedraggled.

But it wasn't all plain sailing on the ark. It was so crowded. Hot. Smelly. Smellier by the day, and you can guess what it smelled of. Some animals stayed slumped in their pens while others plodded up and down, up and down, up and down.

I can't say that all the birds were entirely fault-free. Many sang their pretty songs, but not enough of them knew when to stop. They never know when to stop anyway, but in the great outdoors you can usually escape the racket.

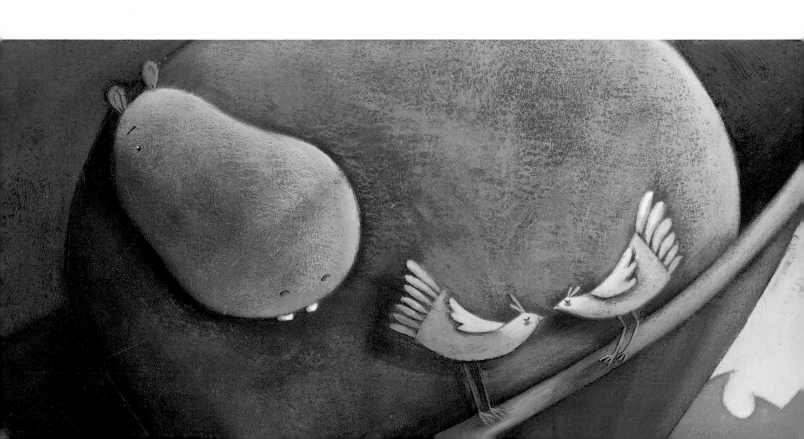

And next door to me were the doves. I know this sounds petty but they are quite annoying neighbours. "Ooh," they kept saying. "Ooh, ooh." They kept it up long after the flood held any surprises. Craa.

Well, when the flood had washed away everything except the ark, we waited. And waited. Then the rain stopped and we waited some more. One day, without warning…

Crunnnnch. The ark had hit something. A mountain top, as it turned out. But at the moment of hitting it, we were all simply knocked off our perches.

Naturally, there was great excitement. But after we'd all picked ourselves up and dusted ourselves down, there was not much new to talk about. All we could see was water… as before.

Weeks later, a distant speck. A mountain top, Noah thought. Then more of them… like tiny islands, far away.

When Noah opened a window to take a closer look, I was right there.

"Off you go then," he told me. "See what you can find."

So I went. My wings just seemed to want to carry me through the clear air. I didn't have to flap… I was just drifting and feeling the sun on my feathers.

Then I lost sight of the ark. I agree I could have been more careful… but I so wanted to find some piece of good news to take back. I flew for as long as I could, but in the end, I landed on a lonely rock.

I found out later what happened on the ark. The week after I'd gone, Noah sent one of the doves out. It could hardly wait to be let back in. Seven days after that, Noah let it fly again and it found an olive twig coming into leaf. When the dove brought it back, Noah declared that was the good news they all wanted.

After that, the flood ebbed away and everyone came out of the ark. God put a rainbow in the sky as a sign of his promise never to flood the world again.

All of that was good news for me and I try not to dwell on the fact that it wasn't me who brought the olive twig. My mate came and found me, told me what I'd missed, and said that God wanted everyone to make some babies.

So we did. We're doing what God wants just as much as that dove did, and God makes sure we can always find enough to eat.

The world needs ravens. Craa.

The Whale's Story

Jonah

Are you a land creature? Then it's very likely you can run.

But even if you can run faster than the waves race to shore… you can't always hide.

That's what Jonah found out. He was a prophet. He was meant to be always listening out for messages from God and ready to share that wisdom with others. Indeed, one day he did hear a message from God, and there was no mistaking it.

"Go to Nineveh," God told him. "Warn the people that I have seen their wickedness. Tell them that they will feel my wrath if they do not mend their ways."

Jonah heard… and Jonah ran. He ran down the road as far from Nineveh as he could get. He ran down to a seaport and asked the sailors which boats were going where. He paid to travel on a ship that was bound for Tarshish – as far from Nineveh as a ship could take him.

But although Jonah could run, he could not hide from God. True, the sailing boat with billowed sail took him far from land and vanished on the horizon, but God was still watching. In the dark of night, while Jonah was huddled below deck, God sent a storm. The howling wind and crashing waves were more terrifying than anything the sailors had known; it was a storm so fearsome that all the sailors knew something was very wrong.

"A god is angry," they muttered among themselves. "Who has made their god angry?"

They believed there was only one way to find out. "Everyone, come here," they demanded. "We will cast lots. Whoever picks the stone of finding – we will know he is the culprit."

They performed the ritual. It pointed to Jonah.

"I can explain," said Jonah. "You're right – I am trying to run away from what God wants me to do. But there's a way for all of you to be safe. Throw me into the sea."

The sailors shook their heads in despair. "But then we'll be guilty of your death," they cried. "We don't want that!"

"It's your only chance of surviving," said Jonah. In the end, the sailors grew desperate and hurled their passenger overboard.

At once, the sea grew calm. Jonah sank beneath the waves and into the deep. He clearly expected to drown… but at least he would drown without going to Nineveh.

But the God of heaven is also the God of the ocean deeps: the dark, shifting world where I, the whale, dwell. God spoke to me, and there was no mistaking it. God sent me to go and swallow

Jonah up and keep him safe inside my belly. There he stayed and there he began to change his mind.

Then he began to wail. "Hear me, O God," he prayed. "Rescue me from my deep distress. If you do, I will sing your praises. I will do what I have promised."

God gave me a new message. I took the wretch to a beach and threw him up onto the sand. Now that Jonah knew he could never hide from God, he began to put his running to good use. He hurried off to Nineveh at once.

That was my part done. The rest I only heard from the gulls that fly all over land and sea. They told me that Jonah went to Nineveh. Boldly, he went and told the people how wicked they were and what dreadful punishments God had in store.

And do you know what? The people of Nineveh stopped and listened to him. The grown-ups listened, the children listened, the great king himself listened.

They changed their ways. And God forgave them.

Jonah was furious. On a hill outside the city he built a tiny shelter, and there he sat and sulked. "The people of Nineveh aren't going to suffer, are they?" he complained to God. "But I'm suffering in this dreadful heat."

God heard Jonah's complaint, and God caused a plant to sprout green leaves and shade him.

"This is better," said Jonah.

Then God sent a worm to chew the plant… and it died. "That's so cruel!" wailed Jonah.

"Are you upset?" God asked him. "About a plant?"

"Yes, I am!" stormed Jonah.

"Well, I was upset about the people of Nineveh," said God. "I wanted them to change, not to be punished."

But I gather that Jonah never really understood about God's love and forgiveness. The very idea was all too deep for him.

19

The Lion's Story

Daniel in the Lions' Den

Speaking as a lion, I don't have a problem with hunting. Nor with eating meat. I'm fond of both and I wouldn't give up either if my life depended on it.

So that's why my story is as puzzling to me as it may be to you.

It has to do with my period of… grr… captivity in the time of the great king Darius. As a young lion, I used to roam the plains of Babylon, where kings and courtiers came hunting. As I say, I don't have problem with hunting… except in that particular instance, when I became the hunted. I think my captors were quite impressed by me… my giant claws, my gleaming teeth, my rippling golden mane. Though they plunged their spears into my companions, they put themselves in great danger by struggling to capture me alive. Bound, of course, and thrust into a cage, but alive and angry.

I missed my freedom. I hung my head in sorrow as I was taken from my own land to the city prison — to join a den of lions kept for the entertainment of the royal court. There I spent many long, dreary days, usually half-starved.

Most of the courtiers were cruel and arrogant, but one stood out as different: Daniel.

"Hello, lions," he used to say. Well, I don't like being spoken to as if I were the palace cat, but there was a friendly tone to his voice.

Sometimes Daniel would come closer: "Do you miss your own land, as I miss mine?" he would sigh. "I'm sure you do. I'm sure you wish you were free to be yourselves, as God intended." I appreciated that.

I think the king appreciated him too; although he clearly belonged to some defeated nation, he did not seem to have any grudge against the king. I imagine he was as honest in his work as he was kind to me. The time came when we hardly ever saw him except when he was with the king. They were always talking about important

21

matters. I think he must have been promoted in stages from a captive to the second most powerful person in the empire.

His success didn't make him popular with everyone. We heard other courtiers whispering about Daniel's role alongside the king and how jealous they were of his power and influence.

"Here's the plan," they agreed. "We go to the king and ask him to make a new law. For thirty days, no one must make any appeal to anyone – human or divine – except the king himself. That will test who's loyal.

"Most of all, it will expose Daniel for what he is: someone who acts like one of the king's men but whose heart is faithful only to

his God. We'll catch him as he kneels at the window facing his homeland and says his prayers.

"And the punishment… Ha ha ha! He who falls foul of this new law will be thrown to the lions!"

I'm a lion. I know how lions hunt. I've watched them conspire among themselves to corner some weakling prey. But that is what a lion must do for sheer survival. These men were on a meaner mission: they were being spiteful and underhand.

Sadly, such people are often successful. It wasn't many days later that we heard a commotion.

"Daniel has been disloyal! He still says prayers to his God."

"Your Majesty, you yourself made the law that no one might appeal to their god. You agreed the punishment."

Darius looked like a broken man as the courtiers urged the soldiers forward with their prisoner. They came right up to the lions' den. They laughed and cheered as the gate was unlocked and Daniel was thrust inside.

I was hungry. All the lions were hungry. But even as Daniel said, "Hello lions," just as he had done before, we felt strangely tired.

I think I fell asleep. I was dreaming of being free again, out on the wide plain under a clear blue heaven. There was singing…

quite like a night bird. It was night-time over the den, although it was bright in my dream. I can't really explain how peaceful I felt.

After I don't know how long, the sun sent a golden beam above the horizon. We heard the king's voice. "Daniel! Are you all right?"

"I am," said Daniel. "God sent an angel to protect me, for God knows that I have never done you wrong."

He waved to us cheerily as soldiers let him out the den. Darius was already shouting orders.

"Where are those men who betrayed Daniel?" he cried. "Bring them here at once! Throw them to the lions."

Suddenly, I felt hungrier than I had felt for a very long time.

The Lamb's Story

The Birth of Jesus

It's sometimes hard being little. People act like you're not important.

I'm important to my shepherd boy, of course. But then, he's little too. We almost got squeezed out of the most exciting story ever.

It happened one night-time, on the hills near Bethlehem. The rest of the sheep were in the sheepfold, baaing in a sleepy kind of way.

I was with my shepherd boy, and we were snuggled between two of the grown-up shepherds to keep warm – only the men had dozed off and were leaning into us like we were a pillow. A bit further off, two more shepherds were awake and playing a game that sounded really interesting… but my shepherd boy couldn't join in.

"Let's count the stars," my shepherd boy whispered. "Let's

begin with the ones that are like a dot-to-dot plough. One, two, three… wow!"

As we looked, the stars began to sparkle. The sky went as pale as when a full moon lights up the clouds. And then a golden someone flew down from above.

The men who were awake cried out – a strange, strangled sound that woke the others.

My shepherd boy may be little, but he wasn't scared. "Wow. Amazing!" was all he said.

The golden someone began to speak. "Don't be afraid," it said. "I bring good news. Tonight, in Bethlehem, a child has been born. He is the great king God promised would come one day. He will put everything right. Go and see: he's wrapped in swaddling clothes and lying in a manger."

And then the whole sky seemed to come alive. There were more golden beings singing and swooping through the heavens.

"They're angels," whispered my shepherd boy. "I've never seen one before, but I just know."

The angel song filled the sky. Then everything went quiet and there we all were in the cold and dark again. I looked around to see the grown-up shepherds clutching each other and speaking quite squeakily.

"Wow," said my shepherd boy. It is a word he uses perhaps a bit too often. "Did you hear what they said? Let's go."

The men scrambled to their feet and began talking in their deep, important voices.

"Well, that was very interesting. Hmm. Don't know what to make of it. Better go and see, don't you think?"

My shepherd boy was on his feet. "I'm ready," he said.

"Let's leave the boy here," said the shepherds. "We'll tuck him up by the gate to the fold so he can just keep an eye on things."

"I want to go too! I heard what the angel said," he pleaded. He was almost in tears.

"It's too far for you to walk," began one of the men.

So do you know what I did? I jumped out of his arms and pranced off toward Bethlehem.

My shepherd boy started running to get me, and then the other shepherds started running to get him. By the time they had all caught up, it seemed silly to send us back.

So we got to Bethlehem. We found a stable where a lamp flickered and went inside.

There was a man, a woman… and a baby in a manger, fast asleep.

The grown-up shepherds looked a bit shy at having burst in on them. "Er… just passing by. Thought we heard a little baby crying," said one.

"We weren't passing by," said my shepherd boy. "And the baby isn't crying. We saw angels, and they said to come and find God's special king lying in a manger."

The shepherds coughed at that and spluttered that the boy had a lively imagination. But the woman smiled at us and beckoned us close.

"I saw an angel once," she said. "You have to take what they say very seriously."

Then the baby opened his eyes and looked at us. Really looked.

Behind us, the grown-ups were talking. I think they were trying to explain about the angels and whether or not they were in a dream.

Me and my shepherd boy, we weren't in a dream. We were looking at the most important little baby in the world, and that little baby was looking right at us.

The Wolf's Story

Jesus' Parable of the Lost Sheep

I don't often come in person to tell a story. I know only too well that in many, many stories, wolves are the baddies. They go about cheating and eating. I'd like you to know that wolves are not always cheats, and that everybody has to eat sometime.

In this story, I am at least unseen. It is mainly about a sweet little lamb. Sweet, tender, juicy – oh, there I go, thinking about food again.

This sweet little lamb belonged to a flock of one hundred sheep. Their shepherd was the kindest, gentlest man that ever there was. He took great care of his sheep. He had given every one a name when it was born and he could tell each one apart.

I can do the same with wolves, by the way. As you know, wolves live in packs, and we know everyone in our own: who's the leader, who is good at running, who needs protecting if danger comes near, that kind of thing.

Well, the shepherd was even more amazing when it came to knowing which sheep was which, because he, of course, is human and his sheep are, well, sheep. Neither wolves nor sheep are good at telling humans apart – you're all so alike.

Even so, sheep do get to know which human is their shepherd. They know the sound of his voice. They know the tread of his walk. They follow him wherever he goes because they trust him.

This shepherd was worth trusting. He knew where the pasture grew thick and lush and green. He knew where he could find pools of water, even in the driest days of summer.

He had built a sheepfold with solid stone walls just that bit too high for me to jump over. He always kept the walls topped with thorny twigs just to make sure neither I nor any other wolf could leap inside.

He had actually built a cunning gate for the sheepfold, too. Even so, whenever he drove his sheep inside for the night, he always lay down in the gateway so that none of us wolves could ever get in.

Happily for us, not all shepherds are like that. Many of them are simply paid to look after someone else's sheep, and they don't put themselves to any extra trouble. Sometimes we creep up on hireling shepherds like that and HOWL.

OW OW OOOOOWL.

You should see them run. Then we have good hunting. Mmm, yum.

Let's get back to the sweet little lamb. It was a mischievous little thing, and not very wise. I watched as it went from one tasty little patch of grass to another, always looking for the next of a particular kind of herb and not paying attention to anything else.

Then I crept closer. I knew it could smell me and it was trotting to get away. It didn't notice that I was driving it away from the flock.

Then I made a mistake. I sent it skidding off a steep cliff in the hillside. The fall left it whimpering a bit, and I had to go miles around to reach it.

Even as I started out,
I knew the shepherd had
noticed that his lamb —
whom he called Adriyel — was
missing. I glanced behind to
see him sending the flock into
the sheepfold. I saw him push the
gate shut and heard him call one of the
village lads to come and watch. I knew
he'd be starting out to find his sheep.

He knew where he'd last seen the lamb. When he saw where it had fallen, he took a really steep path down to fetch it. I saw him skidding and sliding, he was in such a hurry.

Even so, I nearly reached the lamb first. And the pack had come to help me take it. But the shepherd got there first.

He wrapped his arm around it. "Poor Adriyel," he said. He ripped a bit off his coat to bandage Adriyel's hurt leg. Then he laid his precious Adriyel across his shoulders and carried it back to the flock.

Once it was safe inside the fold, he sent the village lad off with a few coins.

"Go and buy some food and drink," he said. "And tell everyone to come out here and celebrate a successful end to our adventure. For my lamb was lost, and I have found it."

Ooooowl. Sometimes I wish I had a shepherd to take care of me. If I had a shepherd like that shepherd, even I'd lie peaceably with sweet little lambs.

The Donkey's Story

Jesus' Parable of the Good Samaritan

When I was a foal, my mother gave me this advice: "Keep your head down, keep plodding along your own road, and try to keep out of trouble."

I've done my best to do just that for years. Donkey's years.

Happily, I have a good master. I think his mother gave him the same advice. He's from Samaria, but his travels take to him places further afield. Everyone makes jokes about the Samaritans – unkind jokes, usually. He keeps his head down, keeps on plodding at his business, and tries to keep out of trouble.

Travelling is what I do. We're hardly ever at home for more than a few days at a time. Mostly we go from inn to inn, and I can tell you that the quality of the stables in such places is not always what you hope. Stay-at-home donkeys sometimes say, "Eeyaw! Luxury inns, eh! Well, aren't you enjoying the high life?"

Inns can be good, but most are just ordinary and some are awful.

My story happened some time ago now, when we were plodding from Jerusalem to Jericho. I don't like that stretch. It slopes down very steeply and the road is rough and stony. It's dangerous for other reasons too. Quite a few people have been attacked by bandits there over the years. Some have been killed.

I was already feeling uneasy when my master urged me along a bit. "Look at those vultures," he said. "They've spotted something they'd like to get their beaks into. Probably some animal overcome by the heat. I hope it's not too smelly."

I couldn't smell anything, and I usually notice before he does, but I had to agree that something was not quite right. I put my head down and kept on plodding.

As we went around a corner, we saw a priest from the Temple in Jerusalem. You can spot them a mile off – well, if the road is straight enough. It's not just that they have special priest clothes; it's the way they hold their heads high and turn the corners of their mouths down.

"Shalom," said my master, as we drew close. It's the greeting word, and it means peace. The priest must have recognized my master's Samaritan accent. Priests don't usually bother to tell cheap jokes about Samaritans. They just turn their noses up. It's because they know Samaritans don't think the Temple in Jerusalem is so special. Anyway, the priest didn't say "Shalom" back. He just hurried on past as if he was trying to stay as far from us as possible.

Then we came around the next bend, and there was a Levite. They help out at the Temple and they always bustle. At least he bustled over to have a word. "You might want to kick that donkey into getting a move on," he said. "I fear the bandits aren't far away."

Then he bustled off. As we turned the next corner, we saw what the vultures were seeing.

A man – beaten up, bleeding, lying in the road. The bandits had even ripped his clothes off him. Those two men from the Temple had just walked past and left him.

My master didn't. He's a God-fearing man, and he cares about right and wrong. He went over and picked the poor man up. He cleaned his wounds and found a spare cloak in his pack and ripped bits off so he could use them as bandages. Then he found some clothes, used the rest of the cloak as a blanket, wrapped him up, and loaded him on to my back.

"Steady as you go," said my master.

I kept my head down, kept on plodding, and hoped that trouble would keep away from us. It was a few miles to the nearest inn, I knew. What if the bandits were watching?

Well, if they were, I think the angels were watching as well. We made it safely to the inn – quite a good one, by the way, plain but clean – and there my master left me munching some hay and drinking from a bucket while he busied himself with the man. The innkeeper came out, though. He's a nice one. He unloaded my pack and refilled the bucket. Heehaw.

In the morning, my master loaded my pack on me again.

He took some coins out of his purse and gave them to the innkeeper. "Take care of that man for me until he's well," he said. "If it costs more, I'll pay next time I come."

That's my master for you. Not fancy like the priest, not bustling like the Levite – just decent. Being a Samaritan doesn't mean he's bad. Quite the opposite. He's a good neighbour to everyone he meets.

The Cockerel's Story

The First Easter

Wake up! Wake up!

I like people to be wide awake when I'm telling a story.

I'm always up early myself: I give the old cock-a-doodle-doo a few times and then I'm off. I like to know what's going on and I flap my way into all kinds of places.

That's how I was able to pull this story together.

It began the day that pilgrims were streaming to Jerusalem for the Passover festival. I watched from the city walls; there was a man riding a donkey along the road, while around him the crowd went mad. They were waving palm branches and shouting, "Long live the king!", "God save the king!" and all that kind of nonsense. There were some men near me tut-tutting about it. That man didn't look like a king.

I watched him go to the Temple. There was a market going on, with caged birds and sheep in pens. However, what made it most like a barnyard was the noise: people haggling, people shouting, people shrieking.

"Stop," said the man. "This is meant to be a place of prayer."

He pushed angrily at a market stall. It fell over and that put everyone into a panic… it reminded me of chickens when they see a fox. Soon the place was in chaos.

The man cleared the Temple, but the tut-tutters didn't like that either. They began whispering about plans and I decided I'd keep my beady eye on them.

After that, things were quiet for a few days. The so-called king – Jesus was his name – came to the Temple a few times. Quite a crowd came to hear him speak. He seemed quite kind, actually. I quite took to him.

The tut-tutters were always hanging around. I saw one of Jesus' friends go and have a quiet word with them. They gave him some money. Looking back, I think they were doing a deal.

Not long after, Jesus came to my house. He and his friends shared the festival meal there. It wasn't much of a celebration, though. Jesus said that there were hard times ahead and warned his friends that they'd probably run to save themselves from trouble.

"Oh, I won't," boasted one.

"I'm telling you, Peter," said Jesus. "Tonight, before the cock crows, you'll deny knowing me three times."

That was a challenge for me, then. I decided to keep my beady eye on Peter as well.

After that, the one who'd taken money from the tut-tutters

slunk away. The rest went off to a garden.

Later, when the night was dark, the money-taker came back with soldiers. They grabbed Jesus and marched him off. Only Peter followed where they went, and even he kept to the shadows. And where did they go? To the house of one of the tut-tutters. He'd gathered a whole bunch of sour-faced men much like him, and they hustled Jesus indoors.

Peter sat outside. One of the servants spoke to him. "I've seen you with that Jesus," she said. "You're not one of his followers."

"Not me," replied Peter.

A man came along. "You are!" he said. "I recognize you."

"Don't be insulting," said Peter.

Later, another servant came along. "You *are* one of Jesus' friends," he said. "Your accent gives you away."

"I am not!" said Peter. He added a few rude words.

So that was it. Three denials and time for me to put a word in.

Cock-a-doodle-doo.

Peter looked up at me. I looked down. His face crumpled and he went away sobbing.

The tut-tutters were getting their own way, and Jesus was in real trouble. When they marched him off to the man in charge of the city, they had the whole crowd chanting for his life.

They crucified him, you know. Nailed him to a cross. Such a dreadful, dreadful thing to do. I watched as people came to take Jesus' body away and put it in a tomb. They rolled the stone door shut.

I don't think I crowed once the next day.

Early the day after, I went to the place where the tomb was. I felt bad about all I'd seen. But there was something amiss. The stone door was open. I could hear footsteps.

Would you believe it? It was Peter and one of the other friends. Peter went straight inside the tomb and the other followed.

They came out, ashen-faced. A woman was there, looking at them with pleading eyes. "The body's not there," they said. Then they hurried off.

The woman stayed, crying. She peered inside the tomb. Then she came out and looked all around. It was nearly light by now and she saw someone.

"Do you know where the body is?" she asked.

The someone turned. She saw and I saw.

It was Jesus. He was alive!

I had to tell Peter. There was a chance to put things right between him and Jesus.

Cock-a-doodle-doo.

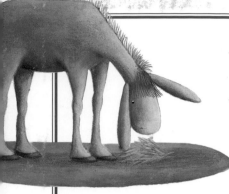

About the Stories

The Snake's Story

GENESIS 1–3

This ancient tale tells of the very beginning. It must have been told and retold down the generations long before it was written down. In this version, a snake plays the part of such a storyteller – and not the creature who was the source of all wickedness in the story. Rather, the storytelling snake is unhappy about evil, reflecting the view of Isaiah 11 that the snake will be part of God's peaceable kingdom.

The Raven's Story

GENESIS 6–9

The raven plays an important part in the Noah's ark story, only to disappear without a trace. This version provides a happier ending. The reference in Job 38:41 about God providing food for ravens is reassurance that God did not forget the poor bird but fully intended it to be part of replenishing the earth.

The Whale's Story

JONAH

For the Jewish people, the sea was a fearful place, a reminder of the dark, chaotic nothing before the creation. The mysterious sea creature God sends to swallow Jonah is a reminder of God's presence even in the places where God seems furthest away. It saves Jonah from drowning and takes him to the place where he can live as God wants and find God's forgiveness.

The Lion's Story

DANIEL 6

Daniel is described as being one of the Jewish captives taken from Jerusalem to live in exile in Babylon. This retelling of an episode from the book of Daniel portrays the lion as empathizing with the plight of the captive. Depictions of lion hunts from the period show the circumstances in which lions would have been taken from the wild for the entertainment of kings and courtiers.